https://www.pexels.com/photo/bar-soaps-over-concrete-surface-7032143/

THE NATURAL
SOAP MAKING
BIBLE

Discover How to Handcraft Natural Soaps Using
100% Eco-Friendly Herbs and Essentials Oils |
Full-Color Edition

Amanda Wilson

Table of Contents

https://www.pexels.com/photo/close-up-shot-of-a-green-bar-soap-4889040/

Introduction

There are several books on the art of making soap, none of which seem to be able to go in depth about a certain method of soap making. Books that only talk about the recipes while neglecting to give terminologies deeper explanations, and books that only discuss very generalized methods of making soap. Therefore, most people end up buying several books with the hope of getting a clearer picture of what they are about to venture into. As such, beginners usually have a hard time understanding the content of these books as most of the books on soap making are too advanced for a newcomer. One thing that sets this E-book apart from the rest is that it is a well-written guide that gives a detailed explanation of each step involved in the process of making natural handmade soaps. This book guides you through the process from beginning to the end to equip you with a complete understanding of everything that is required knowledge for soap making. Included in this book are the basics of soap making, the different type of soap recipes you can easily use to make soap; all of which have been tested. You will be given proper lectures on the different ingredients, types of equipment that are needed for the soap making process, essential oils, simple molds that you can use, and so on.

If you are reading this book, then there is a high chance you are about to embark on a personal adventure into the entertaining field of soap production. Every individual has their own reasons for deciding to make their own soap, however, for most people, the desire to start producing their own soap usually stems from the need for a pure, natural homemade soap. In recent years, more and more people are joining the long line of individuals ditching commercial soaps and other body care products for the homemade and natural variety. Just like the return to healthy and clean eating has grown more common, people are now paying more attention to what they apply to their skin. Thus, the hunt for more natural products continues, as more people seek an alternative to commercial soaps and all their harmful chemicals. Homemade soaps are chemical-free and relatively cheap, made with organic ingredients, and come with the reassurance that you know what you are putting on your skin. People with sensitive skin or skin defects are also picking an interest in homemade soap production in bids to treat skin conditions such as psoriasis, acne and eczema affordably and naturally.

Basically, there are four different methods that can be used to produce soap, and each method has its unique techniques as well as the level of complexity. The melt-and-pour process, for example, is generally a wonderful way of introducing teenagers and children to the soap making process since it requires a glycerin base rather than lye. All that would be left is to add the essential oil and coloring of your choice, and the soap is ready. This method is easy, safer than other methods, and newbies will draw instant satisfaction when they see the outcomes of their invested efforts. The cold process of making natural soap is the most popular method of soap production when it comes to homemade soaps. This process involves the use of sodium hydroxide and water, added to oils and fats, with a range of additives that are completely organic. What differentiates the hot process of making soap from the cold process is the use of heat to burn off residual liquid. However, the hot method of producing soap is not recommended for beginners especially since techniques like swirls and layers can be extremely difficult. Eventually, as a beginner starts to gain more confidence and experience in their soap making capabilities, this tends to be their favorite method of making soap.

Methods of Soap Making

Cold Process

Just as the name suggests, this method does not require heat. Everything is done completely using the heat provided by the oils and lye.

Equipment:

1. Thermometer
2. Soap Molds
3. Whisk

4. Spatula
5. Easy Pour Containers
6. Stick Blender

Safety Equipment:

The cold process method requires using sodium hydroxide lye. This chemical is known for irritating the skin and eyes. Consider wearing long sleeves and pants while using this method. More importantly, you should wear goggles, face mask, and gloves to protect your skin and eyes, especially if you are sensitive to chemicals.

1. Goggles
2. Face Mask
3. Latex gloves

Steps in the cold process:

I. **Select your recipe** – once you have decided what kind of soap you are going to make you can search for a lye calculator online to determine how you are going to balance the ingredients. These can help you substitute parts of the recipe; say for example you do not have castor oil and wish to use coconut instead. Knowing exactly how much to add ensures that the saponification process occurs completely.

II. **Get your ingredients and tools** – Once you have determined the amounts and required ingredients for your recipe, it's time to assemble them. Make sure you actually have all your equipment ready. Clean and completely dry everything you are going to use especially when using lye. Have your actual safety equipment on at this point.

III. **Mold preparation** – Depending on the type of mold you choose, line it with freezer paper or parchment paper. You can use a wooden homemade mold or silicone mold should you have them.

IV. **Water measurement** –When it comes to water measurements, a tiny room for error is allowed. Remember to adjust the amount of water you use if you are going to add in coloring agents that have been dissolved in water so that the overall water content doesn't go up.

V. **Lye measurement** – Unlike water, here we must observe the scale rules to the letter. Use a proper container to measure the lye. Careful not to pour in excess in the jar as its always not a good idea to put back lye in the jar.

VI. **Mix lye and water** – Make sure that you add the lye into the water and not the reverse. Do this in the sink, in case of an accident and make sure the room is well ventilated. Keep in mind that the mixture will cause a drastic temperature rise of up to 200F, so proceed with caution, using a thermometer to keep track. Use a rubber spatula or heavy-duty plastic spoon to stir the mixture. Store it in a safe place as far away from children and pets. Let it cool to about 90 to 110F.

VII. **Fats & oils** – Weigh in the recipe specified amounts. If you are using oils only warm them up to about 90 to 100F. In the case where there is solid matter and fat in the recipe, melt this first either in a microwave or a pot, then pour them into the oils. This will cause the collective temperature to rise, eliminating the need to warm the oils, too.

VIII. **Combine oils and lye** – The preparation of oils occurs at the same time the lye solution is cooling down. This helps to make sure that by the time the solution has reached the desired temperature the oils are ready. Mix the two only when both have attained a temperature of 90-100.

IX. **Blending** –Start by blending by hand, before switching to a mixer for few seconds, then turn it off. Keep blending, alternating hand- and electric mixing, to avoid the mixer from thickening the mixture too very fast. Blend until the mixture thickens and changes color. This state is called trace.

X. **Additives** – If you are to include any coloring, fragrance or decorative additives this would be the time to. Once you have reached trace before mix in any additives of your choice and keep blending until well mixed.

XI. **Pouring into the mold** – At this point, you have what is called raw soap batter. It is still caustic, however, and can burn your skin, so make sure to wear protective gear and exercise caution. Slightly shake the mold or use a spatula to remove any trapped air bubbles. Work quickly to avoid the batter setting before pouring.

XII. **Cover the mold** – you need the soap to maintain the heat it has produced in order for it to cure well. Do not disturb the covered mold for at least 24 hours, and up to 48 hours.

XIII. **Unmolding** – After 24 – 48 hours remove the soap from the mold carefully. The soap is solid but not so hard.

XIV. **Cutting & shaping** – If you are going for the straight forward cuboid bar of soap then wire cutting will be an easy and fast method. For the craftier shapes, special shaping tools are used.

XV. **Branding** – Using a metal or wooden brand, emboss your branding on the soap right after unmolding and cutting, as it's still soft enough.

XVI. **Final curing** – After all the cutting and shaping is done, the bars are to be stored in an open place where they can cool for 4-6 weeks, so they can harden properly, making sure to turn them occasionally. Using the soap before it hardens completely leaves you with a soft bar will fall apart in your hands.

Hot Process

It follows most of the steps of the cold process with a few modifications and a big advantage; the hot process produces soap much faster compared to the cold process.

I. **Lye preparation** – Although not mandatory, sodium lactate is added to cool down lye to the optimal temperature in order to produce a smoother soap. It should be 3% of the total fat weight.

II. **Oil preparation** – In a crock-pot melt and combine oils at 150F.

III. **Oil /lye blending** – Allow the oils to cool down for 30 minutes then pour the lye. Start blending using a hand mixer. Mix until trace.

IV.   **Slow cooking** – Cover the crock-pot and set it to low. After 10-15 minutes, check for a color change. The amount of batter increases in size as it cooks. Cooking time is actually dependent on the size and shape of the crockpot.

V.   **Additives** – Once the batter turns gel-like and even in color; it is ready for the next stage. Add fragrance oils and color, at this point, and stir.

VI.   **Molding** – Now transfer the batter into the prepared mold.

VII.   **Cutting and shaping** – After 24-48 hours, the soap will be solid enough to be cut into desired shapes.

Unlike in the cold process, the soap is ready to use immediately after the cutting and the shaping stage but letting it cure for a few days, nonetheless is recommended.

Melt-and-Pour

Melt-and-pour is the easiest method, and what is recommended for beginners to learn. It consists of using ready-to-use soap base, that just require melting. This method is appropriate for people who don't want to deal with the risk of handling the lye solution. This process is more suited for those who desire modifications for their soaps.

I.   **Soap base** –Bases come in several forms. The best option to start with is the clear and white base. This offers a large room for modifications, just like having a blank canvas. Note that plain bar soap and a base are not one and the same thing.

II. **Cubes** – Cut the base soap into one-inch cubes. This need not be exact, it's only a suggestive size. This aids in melting the base faster.

III. **Melting** – Place the cubes into a pot with a little water and heat to melt.

IV. **Cooling** - Allow the molten soap base to cool to no more than 120 F, as heat can affect the dyes and fragrances.

V. **Additives** – After cooling, it's time to add color pigments and fragrances.

VI. **Molding** – Pour the mixture into the desired mold.

VII. **Curing** – Allow it to sit for 12 – 24 hours.

VIII. **Cutting and shaping** – Unmold, cut and shape according to preference, to be used immediately.

Rebatch

Soap re-batching is basically a soap redo. This is achieved by taking soap that's already made and recreating it to make it better. A soap is taken grated and then melted. Once melted the soap undergoes a process almost similar to that of melt-and-pour. There are several reasons one would opt to re-batch their soap especially if you are selling the soap you make.

A. **Morphed colors** – If you initially made colored patterns on your soap, if they stay on the shelf for so long especially if stored poorly, they will end up morphing colors and lose their aesthetic appeal.

B. **Damaged appearance** – In some instances during transportation or for some other reasons the soaps may be damaged. They may fall and lose their shape. Some may crack for other reasons. Some soaps may mush together and end up forming a single ball.

C. **Lye heavy** –Un-neutralized or excess lye in soap is dangerous. Instead of discarding the whole batch and making a huge loss you may opt to re-batch.

D. **Fainted scent** – Some scents, especially natural scents, can be faint over time.

E. **Makeover** – You may wish to upgrade or entirely remake an already-made batch of soap.

The steps involved in re-batching are:

I. **Sorting** – Sort your soaps according to colors and ingredients If a soap consists of three colors cut, each out to avoid forming a new colored soap.

II. **Grating** – Use the rough side on a box grater to grate them into a crock-pot.

III. **Cooking** –Heat on the lowest setting to avoid overheating the soap. Add water in small amounts, if necessary.

IV. **Additives** – Add your chosen modification and pour into a mold.

V. **Curing** - Let it sit for 12-24 hours.

VI. **Cutting and shaping** – Cut into desired shapes.

Soap is ready to use immediately after cutting, but letting it cure for a few hours or days will ensure longevity.

Soap Making Ingredients and Supplies

https://www.pexels.com/photo/handmade-natural-soap-bars-16244099/

In soap production, two types of fats are used: saturated fats and unsaturated fats.

Saturated fats are usually solid and must be melted before use—cocoa and shea butter are good examples of saturated fats. Unsaturated fats come in a liquid form, and are therefore used to make liquid soap. As a rule of thumb, the more saturated fat you use, the tougher the bar is. Minerals and other chemicals found in tap water are less than suitable for soapmaking. Therefore, distilled, filtered, or spring water is best.

Perfume oil is artificial in nature, and must therefore be prevented. Alcohol and other chemicals found in such oils can cause unexpected problems with the saponification process.

Essential oils are more expensive and often harder to find; however, the amount needed is small (usually only a drop or two). They maintain their fragrance well, as they are undiluted to ensure longevity.

Before use, research the oils carefully; some may be unpleasant or even harmful to the skin. Different quantities of oils are also needed, as some would overwhelm others if they all use the same amount.

Avoid potpourri, fragrant candle oils, and other heavy commercial fragrances, as these also contain harsh chemicals that can also irritate the skin. Whole or crushed herbs can be used, too, but let the soap cure longer to ensure their potency.

Dyes can be purchased in a soap making supply store. Many reports claim that colored pencils can be added to coloring soap and made from stearic acid (most of the pencils are made), but err on the side of caution and avoid using them, as they can

Specific preservatives, such as vitamins E, C, and A, contained in various oils. Sand or pumice can be added to exfoliate the skin.

You are possibly faced with the option of using all-natural or chemical ingredients if you are searching for the ideal soapmaking ingredients. Perhaps you've been exposed to all-natural bar soap and favored its overall effect on your skin to what you used to do.

Commercial soaps typically contain harsh chemicals that dries out the skin. Let's look at the most common natural soapmaking components and compare them to the most popular commercial soap components.

More and more people tend to use home-made soaps as they often contain natural ingredients. This is also why many people have taken it on as a new hobby.

I have to admit that this is why I began my own soap-making business. I turned to a glycerin-based bar of soap when my skin could no longer handle commercially made soap. The chemicals used in commercial soap manufacturing dried my skin and caused its health to deteriorate. Some of these harmful chemicals are sodium sterates, potassium sterates, sodium tallowate, and sodium palmate. Some components in soap manufacture are not made from natural materials. More and more people are actually becoming aware of the adverse side effects these additives have on their bodies so that they use a natural soap.

To avoid any mishaps, know everything you can know about what goes into your soap. You need soap making supplies like lye, fragrance oils, basic oils, equipments, and molds.

1. Safety devices - you will need rubber gloves and goggles to protect your skin & eyes from burns and harmful chemicals.

2. Scale - You need a scale that shows measurements in grams or ounces. Soap making requires accuracy so a scale is non-negotiable.

3. Containers – Your containers need to be heat resistant. Containers should be 1-2 liters.

4. Stainless Steel pots – Only use large stainless pots when mixing the lye, basic oils, or fats and fragrance oils.

5. Stainless sauce pans - A three-quart stainless sauce pan is recommmended for heating the solid ingredients oils, fats, and additives.

6. Silicone Utensils - Only use silicone utensil and molds.

7. Thermometers – Needed to keep track of lye and oil temperatures.

8. Soap molds - You can buy or make your own as long as it is suitable for the kind of soap you are making.

9. Wax Paper - Place wax paper in your molds for easily removal, and to pack your finished products with to preserve heat from dispersing so fast.

10. Tape – To secure the packaging on your finished products.

11. Soap cutter - If you are making soaps in small quantities, you may use a kitchen knife instead. But if you are cutting soap for commercial purposes, then a soap cutter is required for finer and clean edges.

12. Fragrant oils and other additives - these are optional as well. Buy the particular oil you want whilst following precautionary steps; use oils that are compatible with your other ingredients, and that blend well with an

organic soap batter.

Through understanding the different ingredients of soap making, whether natural or chemical, you will determine the one is better for your own circumstances.

Soap Making Oils and Their Properties

Oils are used in soap production and have their own individual properties, which, depending on the intended usage, are combined or applied to the soap base. Many oils are used for their curative properties or their scent or aroma as a moisturizer, skin conditioner.

Here are the most popular soap oils and their characteristics:

Sweet almond oil offers excellent moisturizers and conditioners for the skin. It is also the type of oil added to maintain the soap's state after the trace stage.

Aloe Vera oil heals damaged and droughty skin and is a great soothing agent.

Avocado oil is used because it contains A, D, and E vitamins and has soothing and hydrating properties.

Beeswax makes the soap smoother and is infused with the antiseptic properties of honey.

Canola oil is the most cost-effective option. It has the basic but necessary hydrating properties, although it has less fat, which lessen its potency.

Castor oil can be used along with other vegetable oils to make strong soap that can absorb skin moisture and maintain it.

Cocoa butter is a natural and organic softener for the skin.

Coconut oil can make very hard soaps but is mostly used because it provides a nice lather to soaps once they've been exposed to water.

Cottonseed oil has a calming and relaxing quality, but can easily go bad.

Emu oil any **class seed oils** have soothing properties and speed up the absorption process, without leaving any visible or sticky residue behind.

Olive oil is a costly base of oil that is ideal for keeping the skin smooth, healthy, and younger. It prevents and retains the loss of 45 natural humidity of the skin whilst drawing in external moisture.

Sunflower seed oil contains vitamin E and thus stops the soap from stopping and nourishing the skin.

Wheat germ oil is a natural antioxidant and can rehabilitate dry and cracked skin, avoiding the further aggravation of wounds or stretch marks.

Always make sure to use the proper measurements to avoid any adverse reactions. You may also use a mixture of these oils based on the type of soap that you want to make.

Properties of Natural Soaps

An organic bar of soap is going to be made from various substances that are described as distinctive | completely distinct | absolutely exclusive oils, fats, and body butters.

Hardness

One of the best things about creating your soap bar is that you can control the hardness value. Basically, the hardness value measures how hard your soap is. This means that you can adjust the hardness to your own liking. In order to achieve the best results, carefully choose the ingredients that you will integrate within your soap bar.

For instance, if you want a soap bar with a high hardness value, then you should include ingredients such as, palm oil, coconut oil, mango butter, tallow, shea butter, and lard. If you would like softer soap, then consider using soft agents such as, olive oil, jojoba oil, grapeseed oil, sunflower oil, and hazelnut oil. Lastly, there are other ingredients that can make your soap a bit brittle, like cocoa butter and palm kernel oil.

Another aspect that you should acknowledge is that the hardness value directly affects the durability and permeance of the soap. This means that if you are using multiple soft ingredients then the soap bar might not last very long. The same logic applies to brittle ingredients, if the measurements are unbalanced then the soap might quickly dissolve under water.

Cleansing

The process of creating your own soap is at the very least, elaborate and time consuming. Not to mention that you will be buying multiple ingredients and equipment. However, one cannot dismiss the rewards that come with creating soap from scratch.

You can never truly tell how over-the-counter soaps are going to affect your skin, especially if you are unknowingly allergic to certain chemicals. Fortunately, you do not have to deal with unwanted consequences when you are creating your own brand of soap. Not only will it be made to your liking, but you will also have control over the oils and chemicals that go into it. This allows you to feel safe and confident when you are using your soap.

The benefits do not end here, though. While avoiding unnecessary chemical reactions should be one of your priorities, carefully selecting cleansing agents, aromatic oils, and skin-friendly oils should be on your list of priorities, as well.

As mentioned before, sodium hydroxide or lye is recognized as the best cleaning agent in soap. There are also natural cleansing ingredients that you can integrate, like shea butter, coconut oil, tucuma seed butter, and that is just scratching the surface.

Other natural cleansing agents include, murumuru butter, babassu oil, palm kernel flakes, castor oil, almond oil, and avocado butter and oil. Of course, there are other necessary antibacterial ingredients such as alcohol and benzalkonium chloride.

Another benefit that comes with creating your own soap is using vegetarian or non-vegetarian ingredients. A lot of vegetarians face problems with buying over-the-counter soaps because they include non-vegetarian ingredients. Fortunately, you do not have to be faced with this moral dilemma when you are creating your bars from scratch.

Though the following ingredients are cleansing agents, they are also non-vegan, so make sure to take note of them. Carmine, honey, beeswax, stearic acid, squalene, glycerin, lanolin, guanine, and casein. If you are a vegetarian, you do not need to worry about discarding these ingredients because there are plenty of alternatives. Coconut oil is a great alternative to glycerin, as well as soybean oil.

Finally, ingredients that promote skin moisture are worth looking into, as well. At the end of the day, you do not want a super antibacterial bar soap that leaves your skin dry and dull.

Consider including vitamins such as, E, A, C, and D. You can find vitamin D, E, and A in sweet almond oil. Aloe oil also contains vitamin A and C. If you would like to use exfoliants to cleanse your pores and soften your skin, then add either sugar or activated charcoal.

About Soap Making Oils

https://www.pexels.com/photo/handmade-soap-and-coffee-scrub-prepared-for-spa-procedures-6621308/

- **Olive Oil**

This oil is liquid at room temperature. Olive oil is different from other soap making oils since it produces a mild bar of soap with exceptional conditioning qualities, but with a weak lather. Additionally, it requires a more mixing as it saponifies slower compared to other oils. Olive oil is known to slow down the trace process, so it is generally more preferred as opposed to other oils.

- **Coconut Oil**

This oil is among the solid oils since it mainly contains saturated fatty acids and remains as such to about 76°F (24°C). It makes robust bars of soap with strong lather and cleansing qualities. Keep the amount used between 15 to 30 percent, as more could have a drying effect on skin since coconut oil can easily saponify.

- **Palm Oil**

This oil will yield solid bar soaps with a reay lather and often serves as "soap filler", which will make the soap last longer. The suggested usage rate is about 50 percent of the total oil content used.

- **Tallow Oil**

Throughout the ages, tallow has been an essential fat used for soap making. It produces a bar that conditions and moisturizes the skin well with soft cleansing properties and a creamy lather. Unlike other oils, tallow can attain the most optimal trace conditions. The suggested rate to be used is about 40 percent. However, basic tallow soaps consist of 85 percent and more. Note: The higher the amount of tallow oil in soap, the higher the chances of it crumbling.

- **Lard Oil**

Lard has also been a timeless source for soapmaking oils. The oil creates a excellent sturdy bar with a somewhat weaker lather. Soap that contains lard has moderate moisturizing, conditioning, and cleansing properties. It's a perfect soap filler because it's cheap and possesses good properties that can be enhanced by adding other oils. The recommended rate to be used is about 50 percent. Most traditional laundry soaps are usually made up of 100 percent lard and 0 percent superfat.

- **Avocado Oil**

It produces a mild soap with soft cleansing and strong lathering properties. Avocado oil is highly moisturizing and conditioning to the skin, because it contains high oleic acid and does not saponify quickly. The suggested rate to be used is 5 to 20 percent, since this oil slows down the trace process.

- **Mango Butter**

Mango butter is semi-hard, off-white oil that resembles Cocoa and Shea butter. It produces solid bars of soap with great conditioning capabilities and a stable lather. Mango butter has high unsaponified properties that provide beneficial skin care. The recommended rate to be used is between 5 to 15 percent.

- **Canola Oil**

The suggested rate to be used is 10 to 15 percent. It's perfect for intricate swirls as it slows down trace.

- **Corn Oil**

This oil is not often used in soap-making, nonetheless, it possesses a large part of polyunsaturated fatty acids that make it an excellent conditioning oil. The suggested rate to be used is 10 to 15 percent. It's perfect for swirling recipes, and it slowly saponifies.

- **Palm Kernel Oil**

The palm kernel oil produces a solid, nearly brittle white bar soap with great cleansing properties and a strong lather. Suggested usage rate is about 10 to 30 percent. Excessive palm kernel oil in soap could cause your skin to dry out.

- **Castor Oil**

High amounts of castor oil will yield a soft bar. When used sparingly it provides a strong lather and humectants. That is what makes castor oil useful as a foaming agent in soap. The suggested usage rate is 3 to 8 percent. Any usage above 5 percent could accelerate trace.

- **Sweet Almond Oil**

Sweet almond oil belongs is categorized as a soft oil, and it is best known for the moisturizing capabilities it possesses, in addition to having a strong lather, boosts conditioning and moisturizing components in soap. Almond oil yields a very soft, rich, and creamy lather. The suggested rate to be used is 5 to 20 percent. This oil doesn't accelerate trace but saponifies easily.

- **Shea butter**

Shea butter is a tremendous skin conditioner. It doesn't spoil fast and is very stable. Shea butter yields a very solid bar of soap with excellent moisturizing and conditioning ingredients and creamy lather. It is referred to as luxury butter amongst soap makers. The suggested rate to be used is 5 to 15 percent. This oil also accelerates trace, which is the reason for its frequent usage for as a conduit for "superfatting".

- **Cocoa butter**

Cocoa butter is a solid yet still pliable at room temperature. Its melting point is between 93 to 100°F. It yields an incredibly solid bar with a creamy lather. The suggested rate of cocoa butter to be used is 5 to 15 percent. Rate above that would yield a fragile bar of soap. Cocoa butter also accelerates trace.

- **Safflower oil**

This oil can be used for a white, soft bar of soap with moisturizing and good conditioning properties, including a stable lather. Safflower oil traces slowly, so it's great for complicated swirling. In soap making, this oil is similar to canola, soybean, and sunflower oil and can serve as a partial substitute for olive oil. The suggested rate to be used is 5 to 15 percent.

- **Sunflower oil**

It contributes to a rich, creamy lather and good moisturizing properties. The suggested rate to be used is 5 to 20 percent. Sometimes, sunflower oil is regarded as a cheaper substitute to almond and olive oil. It's also good for swirling recipes, as it saponifies slowly.

- **Soybean oil**

It's often used because of its low price. The suggested rate to be used is 5 to 15 percent. It contributes to soap moisturizing properties and is mild for those with sensitive skin, provided that it is combined with solid oils. A higher amount will cause the soap to go rancid faster.

- **Jojoba oil**

It possesses high unsaponifiable properties that make it excellent for skin care. It produces incredibly mild soap with a smaller lather, when used on its own. That's why it is mostly used as a lather stabilizer, which strengthens the overall foaming agent and has brilliant conditioning and moisturizing properties. The suggested rate to be used is 5 to 10 percent. Any amount above that may bring about a soft soap bar and reduce lather.

- **Lanolin**

If you use the recommended amount of lanolin, it gives soap high moisturizing and good emollient qualities that provide a smooth feel. It accelerates trace, and a more high amount of it will yield a soft bar.

- **Beeswax**

Beeswax is a solid with a melting point of 136 to 147°F (58 to 64°C). That is what makes it too delicate to be used in the cold process. It saponifies slowly, but makes a solid bar of soap with a smooth feel. Beeswax is often used to prevent soda ash, impart a honey scent, and enhance structure. The suggested rate to be used is 1 to 3 percent.

Equipment for Soap Making

1. Scale

A scale is an essential tool in soap making, as all ingredients for soap making like lye, liquids and oils should not be measured by volume but by weight, since that method of measurement is more accurate and reliable. Moreover, volume is not always equivalent to weight. For instance, if you pour 8 ounces of olive oil (by volume) into one measuring cup, the weight would be different when you use a scale. Using a measuring cup in place of scale for your lye or oil will make the end product (soap) lye-heavy or over-oily, thus makes it unsafe. Always weigh your ingredient with scale and avoid cold process recipes that are given in cups.

2. Thermometer

There are different temperature levels that oils and lye could be before combining them. It could be varied from about 125^0F (52^0C) room temperature. To keep track of the average temperature of your oils and lye, an accurate thermometer is required. I recommend an infrared laser thermometer, which is fast, user friendly, and doesn't require clean up.

3. Immersion Blender (Stick Blender)

Instead of stirring soap by hand for an extended period of time, a stick blender will get the job done in a matter of minutes, saving your time and energy. Luckily immersion blenders are quite affordable today. For safety reasons, keep that stick blender exclusively for your soapmaking needs, and refrain from using it for any cooking purposes.

4. Containers for Mixing and Measuring Lye

You will need small disposable cups to weigh out the dry lye (sodium hydroxide) that you need for your recipe especially the ones that are marked to be safe for lye-related uses. Do not use glass containers, as the lye solution could increase to more than 200^0F (93^0C). Lye could eventually etch places in a glass, leading to weak point and breakage. Make use of heavyweight plastic or stainless-steel container instead.

5. Containers for Mixing Soap Batter

I have used different types of containers from Pyrex mixing pitcher, stainless steel pot, enamel line soup pot, to Tupperware pitcher. As the lye solution cools down once you've begun mixing, transfer it to heavyweight glass. 2½ quart container is a sufficient choice. One quart container is perfect for mixing lye solutions and small test soap's batches. Do not use aluminum or any container with a non-stick surface as they will have an adverse effect on the soap batter.

6. Heavyweight Plastic or Silicone Spoons & Spatulas

Always use heat-resistant silicone utensils. Avoid any aluminum containers, choose heavyweight plastic or silicone.

7. Goggles & Gloves

I've explained these two pieces of safety kit before. They are essential, despite my several years of experience of soap making, I still don't joke with them. Wear splash goggles to protect your face from an accidental spatter of raw soap batter. Wear long sleeves, as well as gloves, when handling raw soap batter to avoid any skin irritations.

8. Soap Molds

I use a silicone loaf mold for most of my soap recipes. A quick DIY substitute would be making use of an empty, cleaned milk carton as a temporary mold.

9. Other Equipment

- **Mesh Teaspoon** – It is an essential tool for creating tiny line designs in your soap. Scoop your preferred colorant or cocoa powder into it and softy sift over the layers of soap batter.

- **Strainer with Funnel** – This tool is used for straining herbal teas and other infused oils.

- **Coffee Grinder** – This tool can be used to grind dry flowers/herbs, oats and other additives.

- **Soap Cutter** – Although it's somewhat of an investment, a steel wire soap cutter smoothly and easily cuts a perfectly sized soap bar.

- **Soap Stamps** – Check out the local stores for different kinds of soap stamps.

Basic Base Soap Recipes

https://www.pexels.com/photo/mortar-and-pestle-placed-near-bowl-with-coffee-on-black-marble-table-6621432/

When attempting to make homemade, all-natural soap, it can be tempting to dive right into the more complicated recipes that include essential oils, extracts, and botanicals. So, here are some recipes to scratch that itch. It can actually help you familiarize yourself with the process of saponification, how to identify trace, and also help you to actually get a feel for the equipment and basic ingredients.

Turmeric ombre

Ingredients

1 ½ ounces castor oil

2 ¼ ounces cocoa butter

16 ounces of coconut oil

7 ounces of olive oil

14 ounces of palm oil

11 ounces sunflower oil

2 ¾ turmeric powder

7 ¾ ounces lye

16 ounces water(distilled)

Turmeric Powder

Instructions

Use a lye calculator to determine the water and lye measurements you must include. Mix the lye and water to form the lye solution. Remember to add lye to the water and not the reverse. Let it cool to about 90 to 110°F

Combine all the oils together, heat the butter and fat and add to the oils to raise their temperature to match that of the lye. Mix the oil and the lye solution until trace.

Once you have reached trace before pouring into the mold, add your blend of essential oils. Slightly tap the mold or use a spatula to remove any trapped air bubbles. Work quickly to avoid the batter thickening further before pouring.

Cover the mold and do not disturb for at least 24 hours.

Cut into small bars using a hand wire. You can etch in any desired shapes and add branding at this stage.

Let the soap sit for 4-6 weeks to harden.

https://www.pexels.com/photo/a-person-holding-a-pile-of-homemade-soap-7500307/

Avocado soap

Ingredients

33% avocado oil

30% palm oil

30% palm kernel oil

7% sweet almond oil

Lye

Distilled Water

Avocado Puree

Rosemary extract

Instructions

Use a lye calculator to determine the water and lye measurements you should include. Mix the lye and water to form the lye solution. Remember to add lye to the water and not the reverse. Let it cool to about 90 to 110°F

Combine all the oils together and heat them up to raise their temperature to match that of the lye.

Mix the oil and the lye solution. Blend until trace.

Before pouring into the mold, add rosemary extract.

Slightly tap the mold on a flat surface or use a spatula to remove any trapped air bubbles. Work quickly to avoid the batter thickening further before pouring.

Cover the mold and do not disturb for at least 24 hours.

cut into small soap bars using a hand wire. You can etch in any desired shapes and add branding at this stage.

Let the soap sit for 4-6 weeks to harden.

Tree tea soap

Ingredients

- 45% olive oil
- 30% coconut oil
- 13% sweet almond oil
- 12% avocado oil
- water
- sodium hydroxide lye
- tea tree essential oil

Instructions

1. Use a lye calculator to determine the water and lye measurements you need. Measure the weights and mix the lye and water to form the lye solution. Remember to add lye to the water and not the reverse. Let it cool to about 90 to 110°F

2. Combine all the oils together, heat the oils to raise their temperature to match the lye's temperature.

3. Mix the oil and the lye solution. Blend until trace.

4. Work quickly to avoid the batter thickening further before pouring.

5. Cover the mold and do not disturb for at least 24 hours.

6. Cut into small bars using a hand wire. You can etch in any desired shapes and add branding at this stage.

7. Let the soap sit for 4-6 weeks to cure.

Shea butter soap

Ingredients

- 50% olive oil
- 20% coconut oil
- 25% palm oil
- 5% shea butter
- water
- sodium hydroxide lye
- tea tree essential oil

Instructions

- Use a lye calculator to determine the water and lye measurements you need to include. Measure the weights and mix the lye and water to form the lye solution. Remember to add lye to the water and not the reverse. Let it cool to about 90 to $110^{\circ}F$

- Combine all the oils together, heat the oils to raise their temperature to match the lye's temperature.

- Mix the oil and the lye solution until trace.

- Slightly tap the mold or use a spatula to remove any trapped air bubbles. Work quickly to avoid the batter thickening further before pouring.

- Cover the mold and do not disturb for at least 24 hours.

- Cut into small bars using a hand wire. You can etch in any desired shapes or add branding at this stage.

- Let the soap sit for 4-6 weeks to harden.

Mocha soap

Ingredients

- 25% coconut oil
- 25% palm oil
- 25% palm kernel oil
- 12.5% cocoa butter
- 12.5% grape seed oil
- coffee
- 1 teaspoon of cocoa powder

Instructions

1. Use a lye calculator to determine the water and lye measurements you should include. Measure the weights and mix the lye and water to form the lye solution. Remember to add lye to the water and not the reverse. Let it cool to about 90 to 110°F

2. Combine all the oils together, heat the oils to raise their temperature to match the lye's temperature.

3. Mix the oil and the lye solution until trace.

4. Work quickly to avoid the batter thickening further before pouring.

5. Cover the mold and do not disturb for at least 24 hours.

6. Cut into small soap bars using a hand wire. You can craft into any desired shapes and add branding at this stage. Let the soap sit for 4-6 weeks to harden.

Coconut soap

Ingredients

- 25% Palm Oil
- 25% Sweet Almond Oil
- 20% Coconut Oil
- 20% Olive Oil
- 5% Castor Oil
- 5% Cocoa Butter
- Lye
- water
- Coconut Milk

Instructions

1. Use a lye calculator to determine the water and lye measurements you should include. Measure the weights and mix the lye and water to form the lye solution. Remember to add lye to the water and not the reverse. Let it cool to about 90 to 110°F

2. Combine all the oils into a crockpot to heat them to the same temperature as that of the lye. Mix the oil and the lye solution. Blend until trace.

3. Cover the crockpot and cook on low heat. After 10-15 minutes, the batter will have increased in size, but check for any color changes nonetheless. Cooking time is dependent on the size and shape of the crockpot.

4. Once the batter turns gel-like add the essential oils and stir with a wooden spatula.

5. Cover the mold and do not disturb for at least 24 hours. after 24 – 48 hours remove the soap from the mold carefully. Let cure until completely solid.

6. Cut into small soap bars using a hand wire. You can craft into any desired shapes and add branding at this stage.

Aloe vera soap

Ingredients

- 20% Coconut Oil
- 20% Olive Oil
- 5% Castor Oil
- 5% Shea Butter
- Lye
- water
- aloe gel

Instructions

1. Use a lye calculator to determine the water and lye measurements you need. Measure the weights and mix the lye and water to form the lye solution. Remember to add lye to the water and not the reverse. Let it cool to about 90 to 110°F

2. Combine all the oils together in a crockpot to heat them to the same temperature as that of the lye.

3. Mix the oil and the lye solution until trace.

4. Cover the crockpot and cook on low heat. After 10-15 minutes, the batter will have increased in size, but check for any color changes nonetheless. Cooking time is dependent on the size and shape of the crockpot

5. Once the batter turns gel-like, add the essential oils and stir with a wooden spatula.

6. Cover the mold and let rest for at least 24 hours. Even though the soap will appear solid, curing it for a few days is recommended.

7. Cut into small bars using a hand wire. You can craft into any desired

shapes and add branding at this stage.

African black soap

Ingredients

- 55% unrefined shea butter
- 15% palm kernel oil
- 15% palm oil
- 15% coconut oil
- Water
- Lye
- 2 teaspoons of African black soap mixture
- The base

Instructions

1. Use a lye calculator to determine the water and lye measurements you need. Mix the lye and water to form the lye solution. Remember to add lye to the water and not the reverse. Let it cool to about 90 to 110$°F$

2. Combine the oils together in a crockpot and raise their temperature to match that of the lye.

3. Mix the oil and the lye solution until trace.

4. Cover the crockpot and cook on low heat. After 10-15 minutes check for any color changes. The amount of batter will increase in size as it cooks. Cooking time is dependent on the size and shape of the crockpot.

5. Once the batter turns gel-like, add the African black soap mixture and stir with a wooden spatula.

6. Slightly tap the mold or use a spatula to loosen any trapped air bubbles. Work quickly to avoid the batter thickening further before pouring.

7. Cover the mold and do not disturb for at least 24 hours.

8. Cut into small bars using a hand wire. You can etch in any desired shapes and add branding at this stage.

Cucumber soap

Ingredients

- 15 ounces of sunflower oil
- 30 ounces of coconut oil
- 27 ounces of olive oil
- 21 ounces of palm oil
- 5 ounces of shea butter
- 18 ounces of cucumber juice
- 540g of water
- 400g of lye (NaOH)

Instructions

1. Use a lye calculator to determine the water and lye measurements you need to include. Mix the lye and water to form the lye solution. Remember to add lye to the water and not the reverse. Let it cool to about 90 to $110^\circ F$

2. Combine the oils together in a crockpot and raise their temperature to match that of the lye.

3. Mix the oil and the lye solution until trace.

4. Cover the crockpot and cook on low heat. After 10-15 minutes check for any color change. The amount of batter will increase in size as it cooks. Cooking time is dependent on the size and shape of the crockpot

5. Once the batter turns gel-like, add the cucumber oil and stir with a wooden spatula.

6. Slightly tap the mold or use a spatula to remove any trapped air bubbles. Work quickly to avoid the batter thickening further before pouring.

7. Cover the mold and do not disturb for at least 24 hours.

8. Cut into small bars using a hand wire. You can etch in any desired shapes and add branding at this stage.

Herbal soap

Ingredients

- 25% coconut oil
- 20% jojoba oil
- 28% sunflower oil infused with lavender
- 10% palm oil
- 2% stearic acid
- 15% avocado oil
- lye
- distilled water
- 3% of the total batch weight essential oil blend of fennel, spearmint, marjoram, and lavender essential oils.

Instructions

1. Use a lye calculator to determine the water and lye measurements you need. Mix the lye and water to form the lye solution. Remember to add lye to the water and not the reverse. Let it cool to about 90 to 110 F.
2. Combine the oils together in a crockpot and raise their temperature to match that of the lye.
3. Mix the oil and the lye solution until trace.
4. Cover the crockpot and cook in low heat. After 10-15 minutes check for any color change. The amount of batter will increase in size as it cooks. Cooking time is dependent on the size and shape of the crockpot
5. Once the batter turns gel-like, add the essential oils and stir with a wooden spatula.
6. Work quickly to avoid the batter thickening further before pouring.

7. Cover the mold and do not disturb for at least 24 hours.

8. Cut into small bars using a hand wire. You can etch in any desired shapes and add branding at this stage.

White tea and Ginger loofah soap

Ingredients

- 30 ounces of clear glycerin melt & pour soap base
- 1-ounce Ginger Fragrance Oil
- 1-ounce white tea oil
- 20 drops orange color
- 5-inch Loofah

Instructions

1. Place the cubes on to a pot add, a little water and heat to melt.
2. Allow the molten soap base to cool to around $120°F$. Heat can affect the dyes and fragrances hence the importance of cooling.
3. After cooling, add the orange color and the fragrance oils.
4. Slightly tap the mold or use a spatula to remove any trapped air bubbles. Work quickly to avoid the batter thickening further before pouring.
5. Cover the mold and do not disturb for at least 24 hours.
6. Cut into small bars using a hand wire. You can etch in any desired shapes and add branding at this stage.

Ingredients

- ¾ pounds shea butter soap base
- 1 tablespoon activated charcoal powder
- 2 drops of tea tree essential oil

Instructions

1. Cut the shea butter base soap into one-inch cubes. This need not be exact, it's only a suggestive size. This aids in melting the base faster.
2. Place the cubes on to a pot, add a little water and heat to melt.
3. Allow the molten soap base to cool to around $120^\circ F$. Heat can affect the dyes and fragrances hence the importance of cooling.
4. After cooling, add the charcoal powder and then the tea tree oil. You can add peppermint essential oil as a complimentary scent but this is optional.
5. Work quickly to avoid the batter thickening further before pouring.
6. Cover the mold and do not disturb for at least 24 hours.
7. Cut into small bars using a hand wire. You can etch in any desired shapes and add branding at this stage.

Lavender honey lemon soap

Ingredients

- 2 pounds of goat's milk melt-and-pour soap base
- Lemon zest, 1 lemon
- 3 tablespoons of dried lavender buds
- 3 tablespoons of lavender essential oil
- 2 tablespoons of honey
- 2 teaspoons of lemon essential oil

Instructions

1. Cut the base soap into one-inch cubes. This need not be exact, it's only a suggestive size. This aids in melting the base faster.
2. Place the cubes into a pot, add a little water and heat to melt.
3. Allow the molten soap base to cool to around $120°F$. Heat can affect the dyes and fragrances hence the importance of cooling.
4. After cooling, add the essential oils. Mix into the batter. Sprinkle on the lemon zest and lavender buds as you pour the batter into the molds in layers.
5. Pour the batter into the prepared circular molds containing the loofahs. Slightly tap the mold or use a spatula to remove any trapped air bubbles. Work quickly to avoid the batter thickening further before pouring.
6. Cover the mold and do not disturb for at least 24 hours.
7. Cut into small bars using a hand wire. You can etch in any desired shapes and add branding at this stage.

Scenting and Designing of Soap

Fragrance

There are a lot of fragrances and essential oils that can be purchased online, from your local pharmacy or health food store that can elevate the quality of your soap.

Vanilla, coconut, peppermint, rose, sandalwood, orange, lemon, chocolate, honey, Jasmine dream, cherry blossom, apricot, apple, apple pie, argan, cinnamon, lavender, cacao, mango, acai berry, applejack and peel, apple berry spice, banana raspberry, black raspberry banana, black cherry, cinnamon and cloves, Egyptian musk, grapefruit citrus, Japanese cherry blossom, jasmine, lilac, lemongrass, orange fresh, orange peel, pineapple express, sweet peaches, tangerine vanilla, vanilla butter, wintergreen, and warm apple pie.

The list is endless. You can order any fragrance of your choice online to use for your homemade soap.

Coloring Your Soap

Homemade soap, when made without coloring agents, is translucent and almost transparent once cured. Artificial colors are quite potent. It is important that you use them in sparing quantities. Use different types of colors for different types of soap processes.

Pigments

Pigments are preferred for colored cold processed soap. You can use up to five different types of colors in one batch of soap, depending on your designing skill. It can also be used for melt and pour processed soap.

Examples of pigments are:

- Green chromic oxide pigment;

- Activated charcoal;

- Dried lavender;

- Lagoon green jojoba;

- Ocean blue jojoba.

Micas

Micas are minerals that provide a shiny element to soap batters. They come in many different colors and are coated with other compounds called F & D colorants, pigments or a combination of both. It's particularly useful for the melt-and-pour process. Micas come in a variety of colors. You should use them with care and read the instructions carefully that come along with the colors before using them for cold process soap production. Nevertheless, they can be used to design or decorate the top of the soap.

Examples are:

- Blue mica;

- Cellini red mica;

- Shamrock green mica;

- Yellow lip mica;

- Snowflakes sparkle mica;

- Kings gold mica;

- Party pink mica;

- Desert red mica;

- Rose gold mica.

While mica produces vibrantly colored soaps, batches made through a cold process might fade the color out. It could also turn into a different color in cold process soap production. An example is amethyst purple mica that changes from purple to a yellow color after undergoing the cold process method.

How to use mica:

Dissolve 1 teaspoonful of mica into 1 tablespoonful of isopropyl alcohol and add to the melted soap base. Measurements are 1/2 teaspoonful for a 1-pound weight of soap made when using the melt and pour process. For the cold process you need 1/16 of a teaspoon per pound of soap. For hot process soap, use a 1/4 teaspoonful of mica per pound of soap.

Lab colors

These are liquid dyes which are very concentrated and are useful for both the cold process and melt-and-pour process soaps. These dyes need to be diluted before you use them. There are varieties of them, and they are reliable, long-lasting, water-based colors. They are the most reliable choice for any batch regardless of the production process.

Examples of lab colors:

- Blue nature tint;

- Caramel nature tint;

- Green nature tint;

- Lemon yellow nature tint;

- Pink nature tint;

- Red nature tint;

- Violet nature tint;

- Orange nature tint;

- Azure blue;

- Canary;

- Cimmeron;

- Citrus green;

- Java beans.

Recommended concentration for soap - 8-10 ml of diluted lab color for 1 pound of soap.

Natural colorants

They yield a colorful batch through the melt-and-pour- and cold process, but are less vibrant compared to lab colors. This disadvantage can actually be overcome by using two or more of the natural colorants to create a sharper color. Titanium oxide can be used to lighten some colors of soap which may be produced as a result of using particular oils in case we want a color different from the color imposed by the oil on the soap.

Natural colorants can even be found in your kitchen or at your grocery store. You can also order them online.

Examples of natural colors:

- Activated charcoal - black;

- Alfalfa - green;

- Alkanet - purple;

- Beetroot - pink to dull brown pink;

- Bentonite - off white;

- Black walnut - purple-brown;

- Carrot - yellow to orange;

- Chlorophyll - green;

- Cloves - brown;

- Cocoa powder - brown;

- Coffee ground - black to brown;

- Cucumber - pale green;

- Spinach - light green;

- Turmeric - golden brown to amber.

These colors can be extracted from their dried compounds and macerated in distilled water. This extraction is what will now serve as the distilled water. After extraction, the liquid is filtered with a sieve to remove unwanted materials and yield a much more concentrated color compound. The filtered liquid is now used to dissolve the lye. Weigh out the quantity of the dried natural compound and then pour in the distilled water measured out to dissolve the lye. Boiling will hasten the maceration and extraction of the coloring material into the liquid which will make the process faster.

Designing of Soap

You can design your soap to your own liking for aesthetic, commercial or gifting uses.

Molding and designing equipment:

- Wooden molds which are easier to acquire and use, especially for cold process produced soap.

- Silicon molds which are durable, flexible and easy to use.

- Plastic molds.

- Soap shaver - for removing marks and dents.

- Soap beveller - removes imperfections to give the bar an elegant finish.

- Soap logs wire cutter - these come in different sizes and can be purchased online.

- Build your own wooden soap cutter.

Unmolding can take place 2-4 days after production. Touch the soap to test its toughness, then unmold the soap log by flipping it over onto a clean cutting board/ mat. Use the wire cutter of your choice to cut the log into smaller bars. If you actually want a particular shape, you can get these through your supplier or contact them for more information about soap cutters.

After using the wire cutter to cut your soap log into smaller pieces, you can then use a specific mold for any specialty shaping. Cut an inch-thick slice of soap from your soap log and press the desired shape/or old into the slice. Make sure the edges of your mold are sharp enough to produce a clean cut.

Another beautiful thing about hand-crafted soaps is the beautiful shapes you can choose from.

Soap making is an art, so the variables are endless. If you are creative, you can get myriads of designs just using your innovations and ingenuity.

https://www.pexels.com/photo/aromatherapy-aromatic-bath-bath-towels-206299/

Safety Guidelines

https://www.pexels.com/photo/woman-measuring-some-liquid-on-a-meadow-10536307/

In addition to the equipment and ingredients needed, there are some safety guidelines that you must follow. You will need rubber, nitrile or latex gloves and safety goggles. Protect your skin by wearing long sleeved shirts and long pants. Another important item is a soap mold. A wooden soap mold requires freezer paper while a silicone soap mold does not require it.

Equipment

There are a few equipment safety guidelines for natural soap making. Be sure that you have a scale that works properly. Then, make sure that your equipment is up to date and functional, as well. Lastly, be sure to label all of your soap making equipment, including the scales, so that you don't mix them up with your regular kitchen utensils.

As with any other project, you will need to wear protective gear. This includes protective safety glasses, a mask, apron, shoes, and gloves. For beginners, you can use a wooden box and parchment paper. You should be sure to wear gloves and long sleeve shirts, as well as shoes that protect your feet. Do not wear open-toed shoes. Keep children and pets away from your work space.

You should use heat-proof containers to make natural soap. Metal pans should be made of stainless steel or enamel-covered plastic. Other metals, like copper, will react with the lye and end up ruining your equipment. If you plan to use other containers of sodium hydroxide, you should keep them for soap making purposes only.

Ingredients

If you're looking for a new natural soap recipe, you can incorporate some herbs, flowers, and other plant material into the mix, since other herbs will not survive the soap making process. Whether you use fresh or dried flowers and plants, you'll find that they'll add a fresh, natural scent to your soap. If you're using distilled water to make your soap, you can substitute it for herbal tea instead. Chamomile tea is a good choice for soap making, but a strong dark tea can create a brown-colored soap.

If you're looking for a soap without lye, consider using a vegan recipe. You'll need vegetable oils and natural fragrances. Organic soap will be made from botanicals that are grown without pesticides and have been sustainably harvested. All-natural soaps need to be devoid of lye. A few other ingredients may be beneficial, but they're not necessary. Ultimately, your homemade soap will smell and feel fresher than store-bought soap.

A natural soap recipe must include at least five different kinds of oil. Plant oils are preferred over animal fats, but you can use a mixture of both. Be sure to use non-Petroleum-based oils, too.

Safety precautions

There are safety precautions to follow when making natural soap. Make sure that the soaping equipment is working properly and that you have scales that are appropriate for soaping. It is important to use a good safety mask and gloves when using lye.

Next, be sure that you have the proper containers for the ingredients you'll be using. Metals such as, aluminium, bronze, zinc, tin, magnesium, brass, and chromium should be avoided when using lye as they horribly react with the chemical. Consider using safer alternatives such as stainless steel, glass, or plastic equipment. Run the items under a cold-water stream for 15 minutes, once not in use. After you are finished, make sure to wipe them down completely.

Insurance

If you plan on selling your handmade natural soaps, you should have business and product liability insurance. While you probably won't encounter many of these kinds of claims, you should still have some type of legal protection. In case of an accident, a commercial liability policy will take care of any lawsuits or complaints.

Many soap makers make their wares at home or in a specialized studio. This policy covers tools and equipment kept in one place and any buildings within 100 feet of the property. Your homeowners or renters' insurance may not cover your home workshop, so double-check. All soap makers who are commercially active general are recommended to have liability and property insurance.

Ventilation

Proper ventilation is vital when making natural soap. Be sure to wear a mask with replaceable filters that can remove volatile organic compounds and particulates. Check with your local environmental regulations to see which filters are necessary for your soap-making workshop. If you are not able to use a fan, you can invest in a fume extractor. Always wear gloves and eyewear to protect yourself from harmful chemical agents.

Proper ventilation is especially important if you're working with lye. Lye, or sodium hydroxide, is an extremely caustic substance when it comes into contact with skin or water. If you're unsure whether or not this ingredient is safe for you, consult a soapmaking expert. Mixing outdoors is also an option, provided you have and remain in a designated area. If working indoors, don't forget to ventilate your kitchen constantly.

Once you've made the base, you can start working with the soap. Start by pouring the mineral water into a plastic bucket or large container. Stir the water with a plastic spatula. The water will begin to heat up as it reacts with the lye, so it's important to allow the water to cool down to the right temperature.

Skin-irritating soap

When choosing a soap for sensitive skin, it is crucial to check the ingredients list and avoid harsh soaps with harsh exfoliants or artificial fragrances. In addition, soaps with a fragrance label are not free from parabens, which can cause allergic reactions. Look for soaps with a pH range of four to seven, which fall within the healthy pH range for skin.

It is also important to note that body wash allergies may develop after many years non-reactive encounters. You may experience a rash after using a certain body wash, which is a sign that you have a body wash allergy. Although this type of rash can be easily recognized and treated, the allergy may not be as simple as an allergic reaction. To confirm if you have a skin allergy, a dermatologist must examine your skin.

If you must use a body wash, make sure it is eczema-friendly. If you have eczema, use prescribed emollients as washes. Opt for soaps that are free of detergents, which can strip the skin of its natural oils, causing dryness.

Natural vs. Organic Ingredients

Once you are well-versed with the different soap making methods, types of ingredients, and equipment used to make soap from scratch, you must dig deeper and learn more about the ingredients' quality and composition. The ingredients used to make soaps and other skin care products can be categorized into natural and organic ingredients. Today, the terms "organic" and "natural" are commonly used by manufacturers to lend a rustic quality to their beauty products. They are thrown around as if the terms are interchangeable, which is incorrect since natural ingredients are entirely different from organic ones.

Natural ingredients, even though they can often times be heavily processed, are still labeled as "natural" because it was originally acquired from natural sources. The term "natural" in this context may be referring to the natural state it was found in rather than the heavily processed product it has become. In some countries, "natural" is officially defined as "containing no artificial additions or fragrances and minimally processed." You must learn more about the official implications of this term in your country. Generally, the clauses and standards are quite lenient. Now, here's a catch. Even though you use ingredients derived from natural sources, they may still be infiltrated by artificial substances like fertilizers and pesticides.

To ensure they are completely natural, get your ingredients from a farm that follows ethical practices.

Benefits of Natural Ingredients in Soaps

Let's talk about the benefits of natural ingredients in soaps from your buyers' point of view. They are safe, assuming that the natural ingredients in your soap are entirely natural and free of artificial additions, the final product will cause no harm to the skin. While consumers always look for soaps that smell good and that offer cleansing properties, they often forget to test the product's effect on the skin. Artificial additions and chemicals can be abrasive and harm your skin, making it rougher over time. In some cases, individuals with underlying skin conditions may also develop eczema. With organic ingredients, this can be avoided.

Choosing your ingredients carefully can help nourish your skin and make it softer. They Are Gentle on the Skin some natural ingredients nourish the skin if used in the right proportion. Ingredients like shea butter, glycerin, and coconut oil can provide deep conditioning and leave your skin soft and supple. Instead of soaking up all the moisture from your skin's surface and pores, some effective emollients in soaps help retain water and moisture, giving a glowing look. Hemp Seed oil, apricot kernel oil, and jojoba oil are other natural ingredients that leave the skin well moisturized after one use.

Some products are so effective at moisturizing your skin that they can also be used to wash your hair and are therefore great alternatives to abrasive shampoos. They are free of GMO Certain natural ingredients are made using GMOs and can affect your health. Some ingredients like canola and soybean oil are presumably altered to create desirable cosmetic raw material.

While some claim GMOs to be risky, others consider them completely safe as no concrete evidence of harm has been identified yet. Either way, going all-natural can eliminate all the risks, or you can be confident that your product is 100% safe.

You Can Still Create Visually Appealing Products

If you want to create natural products, you will probably be concerned about the end result. However, with careful consideration and proper research, you can get hold of natural ingredients which can make your product pop and introduce some color on the surface. For example, carrot puree or beetroot juice can add an interesting orangish-red hue to your soap, thereby enhancing its aesthetic appeal. Certain natural ingredients also emit a pleasant aroma that will further attract your buyers. For example, eucalyptus and lavender oil emit a pleasant aroma that can heighten the user's senses during application.

Organic Ingredients

On the flip side, organic ingredients are completely natural and devoid of any artificial or human intervention. In essence, "organic" refers to products free from harmful chemicals and which have been grown organically or produced with 95% organic ingredients. They are free from toxic elements and are not genetically altered. These products undergo rigorous tests by specialist regulations. For instance, the FDA recognizes organic ingredients based on certain tests and background checks. Unlike natural ingredients that may possess artificial fertilizers and pesticides during their growth, organic ingredients are completely free of artificial materials. They are the healthiest and most sought-after source product.

Organic ingredients are gaining traction, particularly in the food and skin care industry. Typically, organic ingredients are recognized by official labels put on beauty products. Consumers with specific needs often prefer to pick cosmetic products that are made with 100% organic ingredients. However, these ingredients can increase the cost significantly. Since you are building a small business from scratch, you may be on a tight budget.

Even though they are appealing and safe, you may not be able to attract clients due to the higher costs. Until you develop your network and build a strong clientele, picking natural ingredients over organic is highly recommended, as long as you remain transparent to your client base.

Benefits of Organic Ingredients in Soaps

Even though natural ingredients seem like a better alternative as the base for your soaps, you should also consider the benefits and usefulness of organic ingredients for a better understanding and comparison.

1. **They Are Eco-friendly-** Organically grown ingredients are free of chemicals that can otherwise harm the environment and increase the carbon footprint. Organic ingredients are bio-degradable and do not add to harmful carbon emissions. In some cases, organic product is also cruelty-free. The tests are conducted using other methods that keep animals and plants safe.

All kinds of skin textures and compositions are taken into account before a product is deemed safe for use.

2. **They Provide a Better Return on Investment-** Even though the initial costs of using organic ingredients can eat up a major part of your budget, they provide a high ROI, making them worth the investment. Since your customers will trust your products (if they are 100% organic), you can still grow your business despite higher pricing. Organic ingredients and products are also useful for local farmers and crafters who rely on local clientele to buy their organic produce. In a way, this can help support the economy.

3. **They Are Safe for Babies** With no artificial fragrances and chemicals in organic ingredients, your end product will be completely safe to use on babies' soft and delicate skin. Baby products are produced using utmost care as a slight change in the formula can affect their sensitive skin. Babies have a high tendency to develop allergies and skin rashes, which is why parents only pick specific products for their infants. Ideally, organic ingredients are safe for babies and the entire family in general. However, if you plan to make soaps for a specific target audience or a different niche, this issue may not affect your plan.

4. **You Can Customize Your Recipe-** Keep in mind, though, that modifyings an organic recipe can prove difficult. Unless your client has particular needs, you can customize your soap recipes and change the color, texture, size, or aroma. If possible, you can also change the shape of your soap to create an element of interest.

If you live in the United States, you need to be informed about the rules and regulations set by The United States Department of Agriculture for Organic and Natural Ingredients, since every state has different regulations.

Here is how four typical label descriptions for organic products are interpreted in the United States:

- **Panel Ingredient Only**: The product or ingredient is made with less than 70% organic materials. The term "organic" cannot be used as a selling point, but can be mentioned on the ingredient panel.

- **Organic**: The ingredient or product constitutes at least 95% of organic materials. The packaging may or may not display the USDA Organic logo.

- **100% Organic**: As the term suggests, this product is made with 100% organic material and is safe to use. The package displays the USDA Organic logo as a seal of approval.

- **Made with Organic Ingredients**: The product or ingredient is made with 70% to 94% organic materials. The FDA does not define a specific set of regulations when it comes to what is described as "natural ingredients". While natural ingredients are deemed safe due to the absence of processing and treatment after the ingredient leaves the farm, the chemical treatment during crop production cannot be ruled out.

Some packages contain codes that show the ingredients' authenticity. For example, a 5-digit code with a nine as the first number is a 100% organic ingredient. A 5-digit code beginning with an 8 is a GMO ingredient. Why Are Natural Ingredients Better than Organic Ingredients in Soap-making? In your case, we will be focusing on natural ingredients as they help make high-quality products with the best results. Even though the use of organic ingredients is highly recommended, natural ingredients make it more viable. In essence, organic ingredients are more beneficial and reassuring as to where the components of your product has come from.

When it comes to soaps or any other beauty products, you should focus on natural or all-natural ingredients. Not only are they safe for the skin (with the exception of any allergen substances), but are also inexpensive when compared to organic ingredients.

When you claim to be using natural ingredients, you are not burdened with as many regulatory hurdles, which is usually not the case when using organic products. If your ingredients are sourced from natural places and the products do not contain any artificial additions, you can confidently label your product as completely natural. Assuming that you are just starting and building your first side business as a soap maker, it is best to avoid clashes and questions which may hinder your credibility.

Moreover, natural ingredients offer the flexibility to experiment and get creative with your recipes, which would be otherwise challenging with organic ingredients. In the end, it boils down to the investment costs, certifications, and legal implications. Unless you are willing to dig deeper and find out more about using organic ingredients in your products, it is wiser to stick to natural ingredients.

Criteria to Pick Natural Ingredients for Your Soaps

If you are convinced and decide to choose natural ingredients for your soaps, it is time to look for the active elements to complete your soap recipe. However, finding natural ingredients is not as easy as it sounds. It takes some research and time to get 100% natural ingredients that fit your budget.

Environment-Friendly Soap Packaging

You can use simple eco-friendly soap packaging concepts to pack your natural homemade soaps. All these concepts are quite simple and relatively cheap since the materials needed are comprised of accessible and affordable materials such as lace, paper, fabric, string, and other natural materials. Since homemade soaps are good for the skin, it will not be a bad idea of you gift wrap some and give them out as presents. If you are thinking what I am thinking, there will be quite a number of homemade soaps and scrub bars on the gift list.

Making homemade gifts can be used as a pastime, save you extra cash, and it can make giving out gifts more personal. Once you've acquired enough skill with soapmaking designs, you can experiment with making personalized bars of soap as a unique gift for a friend.

These homemade soaps can be given out with a small card, place in a small hamper, or you can tuck it inside Christmas stockings. I like to make use of things that look good and natural, both in feel and make.

All of these simple concepts of gift wrapping your own homemade soap can be remade in the comfort of your house with bits of string and paper that you have already. The rest can be easily sourced from the nearest craft store.

Here are some tips for completing your quest and picking the best elements for your soaps.

1. **Read the Label**- Needless to say, before picking an ingredient that claims to be natural or all-natural, read the label to ensure that everything is above board. While reading and learning about each ingredient is highly recommended to make an informed decision, you can quickly learn if the product has artificial substitutes by keeping an eye out for any chemical or synthetic lingo. Even though this is a quick fix, this can steadily help you understand the composition and formula of the natural ingredients in which you are interested. If you spot even one ingredient that seems heavily processed, look for another natural alternative.

2. **They Should Be Approved**- At times, natural ingredients can also be harmful to certain people with allergies or underlying health conditions. You must be aware of the ingredients and compounds of your individual products. Since some official organizations approve certain ingredients, you can use them with complete assurance. If this is your first soap-making business venture, invest enough time, and conduct proper research to be able to assure a sustainable and high quality supply. You are responsible for selling the best products that you can to your customers, as it will eventually affect your brand's name and credibility. Over time, more and more customers will trust your word and willingly pay for your products.

3. **Avoid Products Containing Artificial Fragrances**- Let's say you are in search of a specific type of essential oil to induce fragrance into your soap. While most essential oils are distilled and extracted from natural sources, others may contain artificial fragrances to enhance their appeal and potency. Artificial fragrances are labeled with words like "parfume" or

"parfum," meaning they are not natural. Always opt for fragrance-free products that are free of Phthalates, sulfates, parabens, or any other synthetic materials. All in all, the type of ingredients you use depends on the product's concept and brand values. While going all-natural is highly recommended, you can still use a small amount of artificial ingredients to get the necessary results, provided you be upfront about it. In the end, educating yourself as a soap maker can help you grow your brand and provide transparency to your customers. Talk to an expert in case of any ambiguity and be aware of all the stringent regulations. Remember that the ingredients you use and the guidelines you follow will be evident in your product, which can greatly affect your reputation!

Chapter 10. Soap Terminology

As a beginner, you need to be aware to the terminology that pertains to soapmaking. Below are the terms uses in soap making in alphabetical order

Absolute:

A concentrated highly aromatic oil mixture derived from plants by way of a solvent extraction

Additives:

Ingredients that are not part of the original recipes. These additives ingredients include all expect lye, water, soaping oils, butter, and fats.

Anhydrous

Any substance that does not have water in it.

Antibacterial

A substance that can to fight off bacteria.

Antioxidant

Any substance whether synthetic or natural that slows or decreases oxidation in other substances. The ability to prevent spoilage.

Antiseptic

Any Substances that can fight or decrease infections.

Carrier Oil

Any liquid and odorless plant-based substance that is used to dilute essential oils to be safe for use on the skin.

Castile Soap

Originated from Spain and is 100% olive oil soap.

Caustic Potash

Caustic potash known also as Potassium Hydroxide is an alkali used in soap production.

Caustic Soda

Caustic Soda also is known as Sodium Hydroxide (lye) is an alkali used in soap production.

Cold Process

This simple method of soap making does not require cooking. It only needs heat to melt the oil.

Cosmetic Grade

These are ingredients that are available in higher grade which are approving for use on the body or cosmetics.

Cure

A set time period which allows for complete saponification. The soap becomes mild and no more active lye is present.

D&C

Also known as drug and cosmetics. Once a substance is approved as D&C safe, it can be used in drug and cosmetics products.

Decoction

This is an extract obtained when plant compounds are boiled in water. As contrasting to an infusion where the plant is not boiled but steeped in water.

Deodorize

This is when a scent is removed from a soap product, so the fragrance remains true to their original aroma.

Discount - Lye

To use less or reduce the quantity of lye.

Discount - Water

A water discount means to use less water than the approved amount that is actually considered a 'safe' amount. If your recipe says 100 grams of oils, the water you would need will be about 36 grams. Discounted water produces a harder bar of soap faster.

Exothermic

This is a process describes the heat that is produced in the wake of a chemical reaction.

Expeller Pressed

This is a mechanical process of extracting oil from plant material under high pressure.

Fatty Acids

They are the saturated or unsaturated compound of hydrocarbon found in fats and oil.

Fixed Oils

These oils do not evaporate when heated. Examples of such oils are coconut, palm and olive oil.

Fragrance Oil

It is synthetically produced oil through the use of essential oils and other natural compounds. The liquid product is exceptionally aromatic. Scents like coconut, Banana, mango, strawberry cannot be made into essential oil form. They can only be produced synthetically.

Gel Stage

A saponification stage when a soap batter changes to a warm clear gel, the soap will become translucent, a little firmer, and more potent. Many soap makers prefer it this way.

Glycerine

Glycerine as a natural emollient and humectant is a thick, sticky, clear ingredient produce during the process of saponification.

HP

Abbreviation for 'hot process' soap making.

Humectant

The ingredient that attracts moisture from the environment and also aids in the absorption of moisture into the skin.

Hydrating

Providing or consuming water.

Hydro-sol

The Fragrant water also known as floral water is left over after the steam distillation process

INCI Name

When labeling handmade soaps in Canada and US, it is mandatory to use INCI name.

Infusion

Allowing an additive to steep in liquid for a length of time, for the extraction of its beneficial aspects.

Insoluble

Substances which cannot dissolve in water are said to be insoluble, like oils.

Irritants

Irritants cause disturbing, inflammation or a painful reaction to the skin.

KOH

Potassium Hydroxide.

Lard

Fat extracted from pigs (hogs).

M & P (Melt-and-Pour)

This method is using soap that has passed through the process of saponification.

Milled Soap

Removing glycerine from the soap through the commercial process forms it into tablets, adds fragrance, and shapes the soap.

Natural

A material that does not contain any man made or synthetic additives.

Nutrient

In soap making, anything that has a health benefit for the skin.

Organic

A substance that has not been artificially altered.

pH strip

A paper strip used to measure the pH of solutions.

Rancidity

Unpleasant smell that results from the decomposition of fats, butter and oil.

Re-batching/ hand milling

A crafted bar of soap is grated down, and a source of heat is introduced to melt it until it reaches a translucent stage, then is remolded.

Refined Oils

These are fats and oils that have been filtered from impurities

Rendered

This is when fats from beef heated and melted to remove all form of impurities.

Ricing

Ricing is when a little rice shaped grain forms in soap batter due to the way fragrance oil reacts with base oils

Room Temperature Method

A soap making method by which hot lye solution is used to melt hard oils instead of using heat.

Super-fatted

This is adding excess oils intentionally to your batter to make your soap richer. The excess oil combined was not in your lye saponification recipe.

Unsaponifiables

Uncooperative oil during the saponification process.

Vegan

Free of animal products.

Viscosity

The inability of substances to flow freely.

Water Discount

The process of intentionally reducing the quantity of water needed in a soaping recipe. Not advisable for beginners

Conclusion

Making soap can be a fun and fulfilling experience. The watchword here is caution and precision. There is no one way to make soaps; every method will yield the same beautiful result. Don't be afraid to experiment with these methods.

These recipes are just a guide to stir your creativity. Make whatever modifications necessary, but always monitor with the lye calculator for any substitutes used. You can also substitute an oil with a greater nutritive value for the one prescribed. For this reason, you need the lye calculator to help calculate the adequate amount of lye needed to obtain a good batter.

The process is simple; but first a word of advice: you may not get it right the first time. Don't be discouraged from trying again. With every attempt, you will become better.

To recap, there are different types of soap we can make including cold process soap, hot process soap, melt and pour process soap, and liquid soap. You can color and perfume them to your own preferences. The equipment required, color and perfume, oil and lye you need can be acquired from your grocery store or through online delivery services.

Make sure that all chemicals come with a safety data sheet that will advise you on how to handle the products. According to the old adage, practice makes perfect, there is no shortcut to perfection, but through practice, you will learn how not to repeat your mistakes.

Keep a ledger of your batches, complete with dates and extensive ingredient lists of each batch.

Dexterity and determination will take you to the peak of your ambition of proficiency in homemade soap. Don't give up trying until you get it right.

Happy soap making!

https://unsplash.com/photos/white-and-purple-plastic-bottle-8OU9G0Q53Cg?utm_content=creditShareLink&utm_medium=referral&utm_source=unsplash

Made in the USA
Las Vegas, NV
22 January 2024

84772177R00052